EPIC STORIES
OF THE BIBLE
P R E S E N T S

the TEN COMMANDMENTS
Movie Storybook

Written by Ed Naha
Based on the screenplay

Created by Cindy Bond & Trevor Yaxley
Promenade Pictures | Huhu Studios L.L.C

CrossStaff Publishing
Tulsa, OK
A Division of CrossStaff Media Group, L.L.C.

Huhu Publishing
Auckland, New Zealand

Ten Commandments Storybook

© 2007 by Promenade Pictures

Published by CrossStaff Publishing with Huhu Publishing

CrossStaff Publishing

PO Box 288

Broken Arrow, OK 740013

Huhu Publishing

PO Box 303

Warkworth, Auckland, New Zealand, 9020

Manuscript prepared by Ed Naha. Published in association with Bob Mecoy,

New York, NY.

Cover and book design by Tim Hewitt of Visual Appetite, New Zealand

First printing 2007

ISBN 0-9743876-4-9

Printed in China by Everbest Printing

14 13 12 11 10 09 08 07   10 9 8 7 6 5 4 3 2 1

Endorsements

"*I* encourage people of all faiths to support this Ten Commandments book. I think it is vital that we pass on to future generations the amazing stories of the power of God. It also shows how God can use people like you and me just like He used Moses even with all of his shortcomings."

- Mark Victor Hansen

"*T*his is a classic chronicle, full of powerful parallels to the lives of children in our own time. The legendary life of Moses. The deliverance of the children of Israel. The stone parchment given from Heaven, fire-finger carved with wisdom for all ages of our world. Whenever triumph over terrible adversity is told, this story will be staged again for a generation that never got to hear the wonder of what happened so long ago.

The Ten Commandments Storybook is a marvelous match to the movie: simply told, stunningly illustrated, touched with the magic found so long ago by the original innovator of children's animation; a tale true for both children and their parents. This is such a story."

- Winkie Pratney

"*W*hat a brilliantly crafted and inspiring ministry to children (and adults)! Huhu Studios is on the cutting edge of God's creativity. I love what the Lord is doing through this wonderful ministry and love how after thousands of years, God has remained faithful to tell the story of His friend.. Moses, to our generation through such fantastic illustration and animation. What a Great God we serve!"

- Francis Frangipane

"*I*t was an honor to play the role of Moses in The Ten Commandments. In bringing to life this remarkable man, it was very rewarding. Now seeing the movie in this beautiful book is exciting. I think families will cherish this book for years to come. I really encourage parents to share this book with their children and loved ones because this story definitely needs to live on."

- Christian Slater

CONTENTS

the TEN COMMANDMENTS
Movie Storybook

Moses

Many years ago, in the land of Egypt, there ruled a cruel and powerful Pharaoh. His palace was huge and made of stone and gold. In fact, all the houses of the rich were as big as mansions. All of the houses, the palaces, the temples and the monuments of Egypt were built by Pharaoh's slaves – the Hebrews, the Children of Israel.

Each day, under a blazing sun, the slaves would make bricks from straw and mud. Then, they would haul the bricks to building sites, their skin reddened by the sun. If they were slow or if they tried to have an extra sip of water, Pharaoh's guards would whip them, causing them to stumble and fall. If they fell, they were whipped harder.

At the end of the day, the tired slaves would return to their families and their humble huts in the town of Goshen, a poor place built in the shadows of Pharaoh's great city.

As powerful as Pharaoh was, so too, was he afraid. He didn't like these Children of Israel. He didn't like them at all.

"There are too many of them," he shouted at his ministers. "They could start their own army. Try to overthrow us!"

Pharaoh thought about his problem. "Perhaps it's time to get rid of some of them! I order that the slaves work harder! Harder! Make them work until they drop!"

And so, the guards with their whips cracking, forced the Hebrews to make twice as many bricks and haul them twice as fast. But the Spirit of God was with the Children of Israel

and they all survived. Pharaoh feared them even more!

Pharaoh was determined to break the slaves' will, to break the slaves' hearts. He shouted to his ministers, once again. "Summon the guards! Go out and find every Hebrew baby boy! Throw them all into the Nile! Then, these slaves shall see that Pharaoh is their God!"

Pharaoh's guards were summoned and, as Pharaoh ordered, they marched through the streets of Goshen,

but the Spirit of God moved in the land. God had a plan.

In one hut, a mother named Yogabed cradled her baby boy in her arms while her husband, Amram, guarded the door. The baby's 12-year-old sister, Miriam, and 5-year-old brother, Aaron, were hard at work on a small basket, waterproofing it with tar and pitch.

Miriam looked at Aaron and laughed. He'd gotten more tar on his face than the basket. Both viewed the basket proudly. "This is a good basket," declared Miriam. "It will float."

Yogabed was determined that her baby son would escape Pharaoh's cruelty and live. Yogabed wrapped her son in a Hebrew blanket and placed him in the basket. Under the gaze of a bright full moon, Yogabed and Miriam brought the

baby to the banks of the rushing Nile River. Yogabed gave her infant son one last kiss before she tucked the blanket up around him and placed the basket in the water.

"May God guide you my son," Yogabed whispered.

Miriam ran along the riverbank, keeping the basket in sight. "Nobody's going to hurt my baby brother!" she said.

The river's swift current caused the basket to bob up and down and twist round and around. Miriam, gasping for breath, ran as fast as she could, tracking every move the basket made.

Soon, the basket came to a stop, caught in thick reeds behind the Royal Palace.

10 Moses

The next morning, Miriam awoke and saw Pharaoh's daughter, the Royal Princess, approach the river to go for a swim.

The Princess spotted the basket and ordered one of her ladies to fetch it from the river. The Princess was handed the basket. From inside, she could hear the crying of a baby. She noticed the Hebrew blanket and peeled it back, revealing the face of a chubby baby boy. The infant smiled up at her.

"This is one of the Hebrew's children," she said, as her maids backed away in fear. The Princess softened, returning the boy's smile. "Now, he is mine," the Princess declared. "The gods have given me a son! And he will be known as my son and a prince over all men – a Prince of Egypt. Because he was drawn from the water, his name shall be Moses."

Miriam gulped and ran forward to the Princess, bowing. "Will you need a nurse for him, your Highness?"

The Princess thought about this. A nurse would be a good idea. Miriam grinned. She knew just the woman! The Princess handed Miriam Moses' Hebrew blanket. "This will be our little secret."

Miriam bowed, taking the blanket, and ran off to fetch Moses' new nurse – Yogabed.

The Princess carried baby Moses back towards the Royal Palace and a new life. "You are destined for great things, Moses. I feel it in my heart."

And so, Moses began his life as a Prince, adored by his new mother, the Princess, and pampered by his nurse — Yogabed. As Moses grew into a tall, gangly youth, his constant companion was Pharaoh's muscular son Ramses. Both boys loved to play games and sports. Ramses played to win at all costs. Moses just enjoyed playing. As they got older, Ramses grew

jealous of Moses. Moses seemed to win games without really trying.

One day, strolling through the Palace, Moses heard a strange noise from the garden outside. It sounded like a dog panting. Entering the garden, Moses saw an elderly slave trying to plant a new tree in the ground. The old man groaned under the weight of the sapling.

An Egyptian foreman, as big as a gorilla, began whipping the slave.

"Get up, you lazy oaf," the foreman growled. Moses rushed to the scene.

"Hey, you! Stop that!"

"Run, lad. Pharaoh will slay you for this deed!"

Frightened, Moses shook his head. "But I can explain it to him! He's my grandfather!"

"No, he's not," boomed a voice from behind Moses. Moses swirled around and saw a man, in a Hebrew robe, riding a donkey. Moses recognized him.

"You're Aaron, son of my nurse, Yogabed!" Moses exclaimed.

"She's not your nurse," Aaron said, sliding off the donkey. "She's your real mother!"

Aaron gently approached Moses. Didn't Moses remember the basket? The river? The blanket Yogabed wrapped him in? Moses tried to shake his head clear.

Moses grabbed the big man's whip. Moses hit the foreman so hard that he fell down—he was dead.

The frail slave trotted up to Moses.

Aaron told him that all those things really happened. Moses was a Hebrew, not an Egyptian.

Aaron took off his Levite robe and handed it to Moses. Moses' eyes widened. He recognized the pattern as the same one on his baby blanket. The sound of angry guards approaching echoed in the distance.

Aaron pushed Moses forward.

"Put on the robe and go, now! We'll see each other again, my brother! I know it! I feel it!"

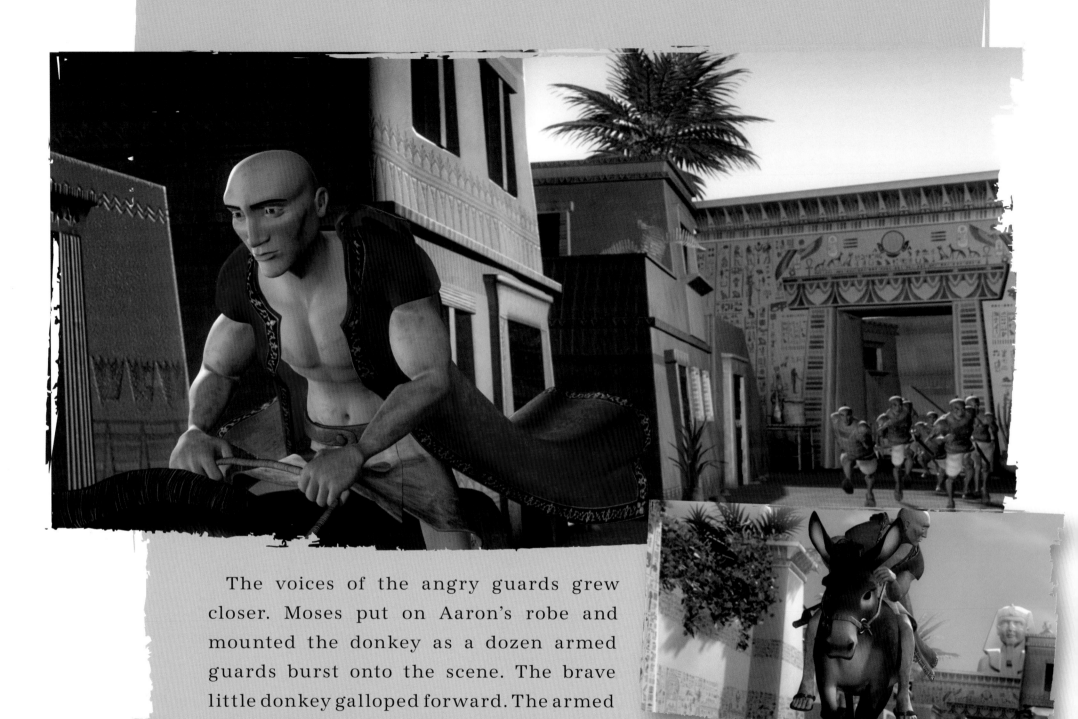

The voices of the angry guards grew closer. Moses put on Aaron's robe and mounted the donkey as a dozen armed guards burst onto the scene. The brave little donkey galloped forward. The armed guards sprinted forward, yelling,

"Stop! Murderer!"

Aaron watched Moses disappear. "May God be with you, my brother," he whispered.

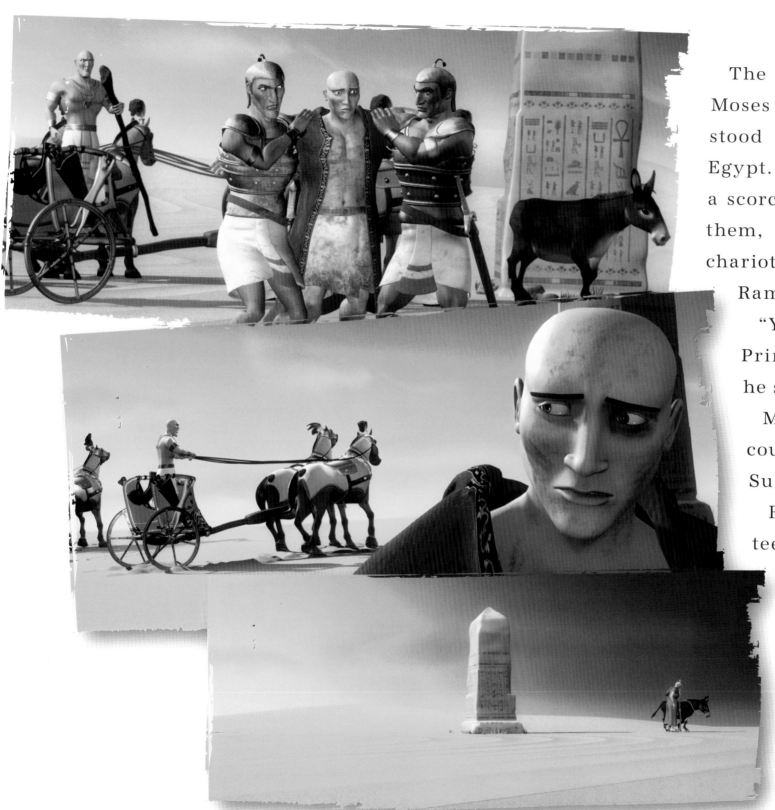

The following morning, Moses and the donkey stood on the outskirts of Egypt. Before them loomed a scorching desert. Behind them, standing in his chariot and laughing, was Ramses.

"You are no longer a Prince of Egypt, Moses," he sneered.

Moses turned to his cousin. "But, Ramses. Surely Pharaoh..."

Ramses clenched his teeth. "Pharaoh has granted you your life. I wouldn't have."

Moses did not know it but, on the other side of the desert, God would change his life.

The Burning Bush

Moses and the donkey soon ran out of water. They wandered in the harsh desert until the little donkey smelled water on the other side of a sand dune.

Moses and the donkey charged up the sand dune, Mount Sinai towering in the background. Below the dune, there was grassy, fertile land. Moses saw seven maidens lead their sheep to a well. They were all sisters. Zipporah, the beautiful leader, began drawing water up for her sheep.

Without warning, two dirty goat herders appeared, pushing the woman aside.

"Out of the way, women," the bigger man bellowed. "Our goats are thirsty."

The women stepped back, nervously. The goat herders stopped in their tracks as the sound of a donkey braying cut through the air. A male voice announced: "The women were there first. Wait your turn...or deal with me!"

The goat herders, confused, turned around. They saw, silhouetted by the sun, the tall frame of Moses holding his staff. The donkey stood next to him. Moses and the donkey slowly walked towards the snickering goat herders. "Who are you?" one of the goat herders asked.

Moses continued to walk forward. "I'm a dead man to Pharaoh. And my donkey has a bad temper.

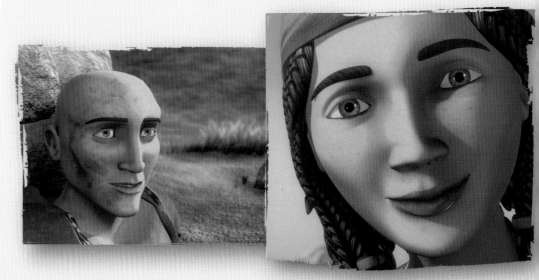

So, why don't you leave, now, and let the women tend to their sheep? The two of us? We have nothing to lose...or to fear."

The goat herders gulped.

The donkey let out a snort as loud as an elephant.

The goat herders ran off in fear.

The seven sisters, led by Zipporah, embraced Moses and offered him water. His head spinning from the heat, Moses sipped the water as Zipporah asked:

"Do you have a name?"

Moses nodded. "Moses."

"I am Zipporah, daughter of Jethro," the woman said. "Are you a Hebrew?"

Moses tried to make sense of his past. "No. Yes. I'm just a stranger in a strange land."

The seven sisters led Moses and the donkey towards the massive tent of their father, Jethro.

Jethro soon gave Moses his daughter Zipporah as a wife.

And Moses and Zipporah had two sons. After a while, a happy Moses nearly forgot his old life in Egypt.

But back in Egypt, the Children of Israel still suffered under the whips of Ramses. The people cried out for God to help them. And God heard their cries. And God decided to pay Moses a visit and set His Divine Plan into motion.

One fine day, Moses, herded a flock of sheep through a pasture. One little lamb bolted from the herd, heading towards Mount Sinai. The lamb reached the mountain and began trotting up a pathway. Moses ran behind it.

"Little one! Wait!"

Moses reached a small ledge. He couldn't believe his eyes. Before him was a burning bush. The fire was bright and powerful, yet it did not burn the bush's branches or leaves. Moses gulped and walked towards the bush. He stopped, startled, when a warm fatherly voice arose from within the flames. It was the voice of God.

22   The Burning Bush

"Moses. Moses," said the voice.

Moses nervously raised his hand as a child would to a teacher.

"I'm here. I'm right here."

"Take off your shoes, for you are standing on holy ground," advised the voice.

Moses quickly turned away from the bush, trembling. He took off his sandals, awaiting the worst. He took a deep breath and faced the burning bush.

The voice identified itself. "I am the God of your fathers, the God of Abraham and the God of Isaac and the God of Jacob."

Moses was surprised. This couldn't be happening! Yet, it was!

God continued to speak. "I have seen the affliction of my people who are in Egypt. I have heard their cries. I know their sorrows. Therefore, I will send you, Moses to free them. You will bring my people to serve me upon this mountain."

Moses thought about this. He knew what the Egyptians were like. "Lord," he said. "They're going to need more than my word."

So God told Moses to take his shepherd's staff and throw it onto the ground. Moses did as he was told. Immediately when his staff hit the ground, it was transformed into a large, poisonous serpent! Moses gasped.

God then told Moses to pick up the snake by its tail. Moses trembled but obeyed God. He snatched the large snake by its tail. As soon as he did so, the snake was transformed back into a shepherd's staff. Moses grabbed the staff and smiled.

God told Moses to show the people such signs and they would believe.

In an instant, the fire disappeared from the bush. Moses hesitated before walking forward. He studied the shrub. Not a single leaf nor branch had been burned. He glanced from the bush to his shepherd's staff. Truly, he had been in the presence of God.

That night, as a full moon shone over Mount Sinai, Moses packed the last of his belongings on his donkey. He said tearful farewell to his family and started off on the long trek back to Egypt. He prayed to God to remain strong. He knew that Pharaoh would not be glad to see him.

Moses Returns to Egypt

Flickering torch held high, Moses led his donkey through vast foothills leading back towards Egypt. It was like walking through a maze.

A voice whispered. "Moses? Is that you?"

Aaron stepped out of the shadows, grinning. The two brothers embraced. Aaron told Moses that, in a dream, he heard God tell him to meet Moses here.

"That wasn't a dream." Moses replied. God had a mission for them both.

"We go to Pharaoh?" Aaron asked.

Moses nodded. Aaron was not very happy. Egypt had a new Pharaoh now. Ramses was the new ruler of Egypt.

The brothers entered the town of Goshen and headed for a particular hut. The door swung open and there stood Moses' sister Miriam.

"Welcome back, baby brother," she exclaimed.

"It's good to finally be home," Moses smiled.

He stared past her. The hut was crowded with older men. Miriam laughed. "The elders all want to hear what God has told you."

Moses rolled his eyes as Miriam led him forward. Moses hated to speak before crowds...even little ones.

The following morning, Moses and Aaron stood anxiously before the Royal Palace. Moses, holding his staff, requested an audience with Ramses. The Royal guards pointed their spears at the brothers. "Pharaoh doesn't see Hebrews," one guard sneered.

At that point, Ramses, galloped up in his hunting chariot, surrounded by guards.

Ramses thought it might be amusing to hear what Moses had to say. He brushed Moses and Aaron aside and said to his guards. "Let them both wait until all the incense in the palace has been lit. It will cover their stench."

Moses Returns to Egypt

Later, in the Royal Palace, Ramses sat on his towering throne. A half-dozen Royal Ministers and four Court Magicians — all holding golden staffs — stood behind him. Leaning against Ramses' throne was his eight-year-old son. Ramses listened to Moses' tale and frowned. His son, seeing his father's anger, frowned as well. Moses finished his speech by stating: "And as was told to me, the Lord God of Israel says... Let My people go!"

Ramses' face grew red. "You expect me to just let the Hebrews leave? Just like that? Because a God I do not know, have never heard of, wants me to? You've been in the desert too long. Look at you, with your old robe and your splintered staff. You are pathetic in my eyes. But, then, you've always been pathetic. A murderer. A coward. A fraud. As for your Lord God?"

Ramses leaned forward. "Pharaoh is the God of Egypt. There is no other!"

Moses stood silently. He remembered what God told him on the mountain. He raised his staff and said:

"Behold the power of the Lord God!" He threw down his staff onto the floor.

...staff became a gigantic snake. ...ses' son was afraid. Ramses laughed, patting his son's head. "It's just a trick, my son. Watch and see."

Ramses snapped his fingers. His magicians stepped forward and threw their golden staffs upon the floor. The magicians' golden staffs turned into snakes, as well. Ramses laughed at Moses.

"Even my magicians can out-do your so-called God," he sneered.

Moses smiled at Ramses, not bothering to look at the floor. The magicians gasped. Ramses' mouth dropped open.

Ramses' son held on tight to his father. On the floor, Moses' serpent lashed out at the magicians' snakes. It ate them, one by one. Moses stepped forward and grabbed his serpent by the tail. It transformed itself back into a shepherd's staff.

Angry, Ramses jumped out of his throne and ran up to Moses. Moses was not afraid. "Here me, Ramses," Moses said. "The Lord God has commanded it. Let my people go."

Ramses clenched his teeth. "Tell your God that Pharaoh will not release his slaves. They barely work as it is. Tell your God that I will increase their work. I will no longer give them straw to make bricks. They must find their own straw and, if they don't make enough bricks? They will die by day's end. Tell your God that, Moses!"

Pharaoh's orders traveled quickly. Heavily armed taskmasters whipped the Hebrew slaves as the tired men pulled wagons, only half-filled with bricks. The whips cracked. The slaves moaned.

"Anyone who doesn't make enough bricks dies at sundown," yelled one taskmaster. "More bricks! More bricks!"

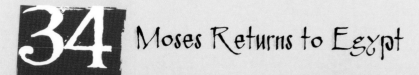

Moses and Aaron were saddened by the sight. A group of angry slaves, led by one of Pharaoh's spies, ran up to the brothers. The spy, a Hebrew named Dathan, shoved a finger in Moses' chest. "Are you happy, now? They're working us to death."

"Maybe you didn't hear God correctly," Dathan explained. "Maybe you got it all wrong. Go tell Pharaoh you made a mistake. Apologize, now!"

The Plagues

Moses found a secluded spot and dropped down onto his knees. He faced the sky. "Lord God," he whispered. "I did everything you told me but I've only made things worse."

A wind surrounded Moses and God spoke to him. "Tomorrow, go again to Pharaoh. I will make you like a god to him. Take your staff and stretch it over the river. You shall multiply my wonders in this land. All will know that I am the Lord!" The wind faded away, as did the voice of God.

The following day, Moses and Aaron stood on a path next to the Nile River. Pharaoh and his royal guards, on horses, galloped forward. Moses raised his staff and looked up at Ramses.

"Pharaoh," he said, "the Lord God has commanded you to let my people go."

Ramses roared with laughter. "Move or I'll trample you, Moses."

"Behold His power!" Moses shouted. He lifted his staff high into the air and brought it down upon the Nile. The water in the river turned to blood. All across Egypt the waters turned to blood and the fish died. The river stank. People could not bathe. People could not drink.

Pharaoh didn't care. "More magic, Moses? I don't need to drink water. I have wine."

Moses stood tall. "You heart is hard, Pharaoh, but God is stronger. He has instructed me. I will show you that He is the one true God!"

Moses softened, "Ramses, please. Let my people go. I fear that many of your people will suffer. Some will die."

Ramses was unmoved. "Pharaoh is

the only god you have to fear, Moses," Ramses shouted. "You'll be the one to die!"

Aaron gulped as Moses raised his staff into the air again. Moses' staff struck the dirt. A whirlwind of sand and dust formed. It grew bigger and bigger and bigger. The dust turned to lice. The hungry insects swarmed at Pharaoh and his guards. Their horses snorted and galloped off.

The lice spread across Egypt. Pharaoh's magicians could do nothing. There were lice upon man and beast. Moses was sure Ramses would send for him. But Ramses did not.

Later, alone in a quiet spot, Moses prayed to God. "Pharaoh hears, but does not listen, Lord."

God whispered to Moses. Moses nodded, stood and raised his staff skyward.

At the Royal Palace, surprised guards ran up the stairway. An army of frogs jumped up the steps and then died. All over Egypt, frogs jumped out of rivers and streams and spread all over the land. They entered houses, jumping through windows. They even entered the Royal Palace. Soon, all the frogs died, creating a very bad smell.

On his throne, Ramses comforted his frightened son. "This is all Moses' God has to torment me? Frogs?" Ramses laughed as his servants swept away the dead frogs in the throne room. His son laughed as well.

unmoved, stood on a hill above the Royal City and raised his staff towards the sky again!

Down below, the rich Egyptians felt the wrath of God. Their faces and arms began to bubble. Large boils covered their bodies. The more the Egyptians scratched at them, the more the boils spread. They ran screaming down the street, passing a group of Hebrew slaves pulling wagons of bricks. The Hebrews' skin was fine. Only the Egyptians were stricken. Ramses was unmoved.

In a field, alone, Moses raised his staff towards the heavens again. Across the field, a cloud of biting flies suddenly attacked a group of Egyptians tending their cattle! Clouds of flies covered the land. The cattle died. The land stank.

"Moses does bad tricks!" Ramses' son declared.

Ramses laughed out loud.

"Exactly! Bad tricks and nothing more."

Moses, seeing that Pharaoh was

Moses again raised his staff towards Heaven. The Lord rained hail upon the Egyptians. As the hail hit the ground, it burst into flame. The Egyptians walking on the streets caught fire. All the streets burst into flame. Only the Hebrews and their homes and their fields were spared.

But Pharaoh was unmoved. So, God sent waves of locusts down to destroy the Egyptians' crops. But Pharaoh ignored the latest sign from God.

So, God sent darkness to the land of Egypt. The Royal City was plunged into the darkness of night. Yet, it was daytime. Black clouds swirled in the sky like ocean waves. Thunder rumbled. Citizens ran for their homes. All plants and flowers that needed the sun withered and died. For three entire days, Egypt was covered in blackness. Only the Hebrews in Goshen saw the light of day.

Ramses heaved a giant sigh. "Bring me Moses."

Later, Moses slowly walked up the Palace steps, staff in hand. Ramses' voice was low, almost a growl. "Take this death from my kingdom," he said to Moses. Moses nodded. He raised his staff and spread his arms. The thunder stopped. Sunlight poured into the Royal Palace and spread throughout the land of Egypt.

"Pharaoh," Moses said. "How long will you wait before you see that this is all God's will? You've seen what the Lord God can do! Don't think that you are greater than God!"

Ramses stared at Moses. "Who is this God of yours, Moses?"

"The Lord God of Abraham and of Isaac and of Jacob," Moses answered.

"His name!" Ramses yelled. "I want his name!"

"Yahweh," Moses whispered.

"I know not such a name," Ramses said.

He shooed Moses away. "If you don't want to see your people slain, Leave this house!"

Moses grew angry.

"The Lord will bring one more plague upon Egypt," he stated. "Tonight, at midnight, the Lord will descend upon your kingdom and kill every firstborn child, from the rich to the poor. Only the children of Israel will be spared. Tomorrow, you shall set my people free as your own people weep and ask: 'Why didn't Pharaoh listen to The Lord God?'"

Ramses ran down to Moses in anger. "You are banished from this house! You will never see my face again, until the day I kill you!"

Moses smiled sadly and left the Palace. "I will mourn your loss, Ramses."

Ramses was left alone with his trembling son. He was suddenly afraid. Ramses' son was the first born into the royal family.

Moses gathered all the Hebrew elders of Goshen and told them that God had spoken to him. This day was the beginning of their journey to the Promised Land.

When Death roamed the land, it would see the mark of lamb's blood on the Hebrews' doors. Seeing that sign, it would pass over the Hebrews' homes. Death would harm no Hebrew whose door was marked. But, in years to come, Moses said that all Hebrews must celebrate this night — this night of the Passover.

The elders bowed their heads and ran off to spread the word throughout Goshen. And the people did as the Lord commanded.

That night, all Hebrews must eat nothing but unleavened bread and the meat of lamb. Every Hebrew must take the blood of that lamb and spread it on their front doors. They must not leave their homes until morning.

For that night, the Lord God would come to Egypt. God Himself would deal with the Egyptians but He would protect the Hebrews from Death, the Destroyer.

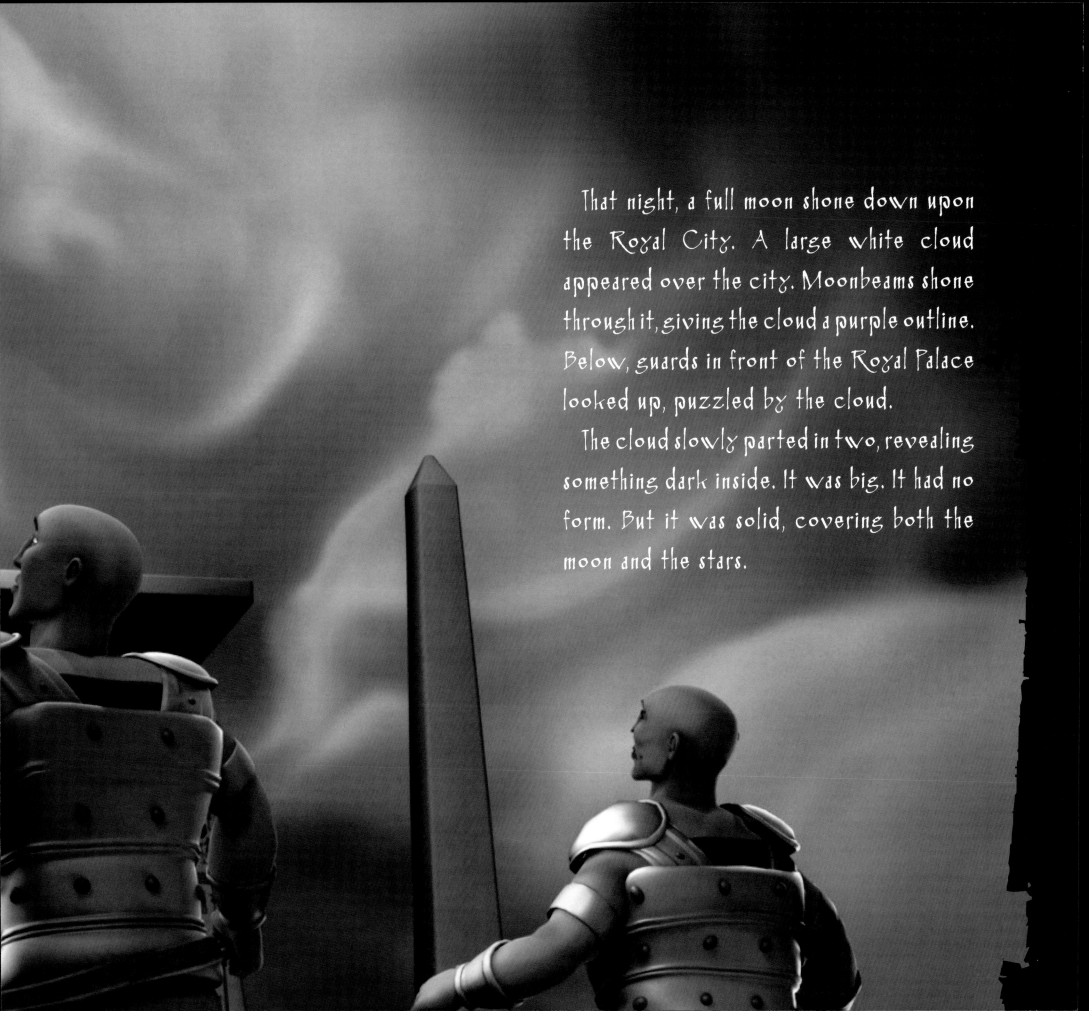

That night, a full moon shone down upon the Royal City. A large white cloud appeared over the city. Moonbeams shone through it, giving the cloud a purple outline. Below, guards in front of the Royal Palace looked up, puzzled by the cloud.

The cloud slowly parted in two, revealing something dark inside. It was big. It had no form. But it was solid, covering both the moon and the stars.

From within the darkness, swarms of other dark things emerged, flying and howling. The swarms whirled and twirled and flew down towards the Royal City.

The shadow shapes floated down the streets of the City, moaning and sighing. In Goshen, the dark forms flew towards the Hebrews' homes. Spotting the blood marks on the doors and recognizing that these homes were blessed by God, the shadows moved on.

In Aaron's home, Moses sat with his brother and his sister, Miriam. He felt a sudden chill and heard a faint whisper.

"What is it?" Miriam asked.

"Death has just passed us by," Moses replied.

At the Royal Palace, terrified guards ran away from the building as the shadow shapes swooped down.

From inside the Palace, the voice of Ramses thundered. "Oh, great god Ra! No! Not my son! Not my son! Find Moses! Get me Moses! Moses!"

The next day, the sun shone down on the Royal Palace. The building's huge stone columns were cracked. The place was in ruins. Inside, Ramses sat on his throne. His little boy's body was draped upon his knees. Ramses talked to himself. "All the Hebrews of Goshen were spared."

He heard footsteps and looked up. Moses stood before him.

Moses was saddened. "I'm so sorry."

Ramses didn't move. He whispered. "Say nothing to me."

Moses said nothing.

Finally, Ramses shouted: "Go! Take your people and go! Take our riches! I don't care! Serve your God and be gone!"

Moses nodded. "We will go. The sons and daughters, the young and the old, the flocks and the herds. We all have seen that the Lord God lives."

Before Moses could leave, Ramses said in an evil, even voice. "Moses. I will never forget what you have done to me...and my kingdom."

The Red Sea

The noon sun shone down on an amazing sight. Hundreds of thousands of Hebrews were leaving the Royal City. At the head of the procession, Moses marched, staff in hand. Miriam and Aaron walked at his side.

"God has blessed you, my brother," said Miriam.

Moses smiled. "God has blessed us all. Remember this day. This day, the hand of the Lord broke the chains of slavery."

Aaron spoke up. "Moses? Where is this Promised Land?"

Moses shrugged his shoulders. "I don't know."

"No map to guide us?" Miriam asked.

Moses beamed. "He will guide us. I have faith that He will lead the way."

As Moses finished speaking a gigantic pillar of cloud appeared before the Hebrews. It drifted along the desert floor.

nd God led the Children of Israel. During the day, He appeared as a pillar of cloud. At night, He appeared as a pillar of fire.

After several days, Moses and his people reached the banks of the Red Sea. The sea was vast, with huge waves hitting the shoreline.

Moses turned to those in the crowd stretching endlessly behind him.

"We camp here!"

The people in the crowd were puzzled, but they obeyed Moses. Miriam leaned over to Moses. "Has God told you how we are to cross this large sea?"

Moses shrugged. "Not exactly."

Miriam glanced over her shoulder at the countless number of Hebrews behind them. "I wouldn't let too many people know that," she whispered to Moses.

 The Red Sea

Far off in the Royal City, an angry Ramses sat on his throne. Two of his ministers stood nervously before him.

"Our farms die," Ramses muttered. "Our buildings are not being built. There's no one to tend our herds."

He raised his head towards his ministers and shouted: "Why have you set all the slaves free?"

The first minister gulped. "You ordered it, Great Pharaoh. After their God killed all…"

Ramses slammed a fist down upon his throne. "I was a fool! It was a moment of weakness. Summon the chariots! We will pursue the Hebrews!

At the banks of the Red Sea, the Hebrews watched the sun set. Suddenly a panicked voice shouted: "Pharaoh is coming! Pharaoh is coming."

Moses stood on a huge boulder overlooking the Sea.

"What kind of a leader are you?" Dathan shouted. "You've led us into the wilderness to die! You've led us into a trap! We can't fight Pharaoh."

In the setting sun's red glow, Ramses and his entire army appeared on the top of a far off sand dune, ready to charge.

Moses spoke to the Children of Israel. "Pack your things. Be ready to move."

"The Lord shall fight for you," Moses answered.

High above the Red Sea, Ramses raised his sword to his charioteers and shouted: "At my command! We attack! Show no mercy!"

"Where's your God, now, Moses?" Ramses thought.

Without warning, a huge pillar of fire erupted in front of the Egyptian soldiers. It swirled like a tornado, held in place by the hand of God.

Tongues of fire lashed out at the charging Egyptians.

There was no way the charioteers could make it to the Red Sea. Ramses remained calm, thinking: "Moses, you cannot stop me. You will die at my hands."

Moses stared at the Red Sea. He turned towards his people.

"The Egyptians you see today, you will never see again. Behold how the Lord protects you!" Moses shouted.

Moses raised his staff. A howling wind arose, the frightened Hebrews clung to each other. As they stared at the water. It began to rise and fall wildly, bubbling as if it were boiling. Waves began to shoot out of the sea. Each wave was as big as a skyscraper.

Leaning into the wind, Moses held his staff higher.

The Hebrews gasped as, the Red Sea rose higher and higher. It began to part in two. Two great, endless walls of water soared up to the heavens and remained in place.

Between the two watery walls was a wide path of dry land.

Moses smiled and waved the astonished Hebrews on. "Go!" he cried. "Go!"

The caravan of people continued onward. They gazed at the great walls of water. Behind the walls, they could see fish and sea creatures swim. High above, on the sand dune, Ramses watched in awe as the Hebrews crossed the dry seabed.

He stared at the pillar of fire separating him from the Hebrews. The pillar of fire began to shrink. It evaporated, giving Ramses and his charioteers a clear path to the Hebrews.

As Moses raised his staff higher, the two towering walls of the sea began to shimmy and shake. The waves rushed forward towards Pharaoh's army as the walls of water crashed down. A tidal wave of churning water covered both the dry path and the charioteers. They were brushed aside like ants, sinking beneath the swirling sea.

"Attack!" Ramses called, waving his sword and urging his horse onward. Ramses felt something jolt his chariot. One of the wheels hit a rock. His horse broke free. Ramses' chariot rolled and rolled. Ramses struggled and got to his knees. He faced the

Red Sea. His army charged down the dry path between the two towering walls of water.

Moses watched Pharaoh's charioteers gallop forward. He raised his staff, glancing at the Hebrews. "Do not be afraid. Behold the salvation of the Lord."

On his sand dune, Ramses watched, horrified, as his entire army disappeared beneath the waves. Sobbing, he turned his back on the Red Sea. He started his long walk home back to the Royal City, back to the broken land of Egypt.

Watching the army disappear from his side of the Sea, Moses raised both arms and faced the sky. "There is no one like you, Lord!"

"Now, on to the Promised Land!"

The Desert Journey

Moses and his people followed the cloud pillar deeper and deeper into the desert. The land was hot and barren of life. The people walked many days and found no water. "What kind of a trip is this?" Dathan groused. "No food? No water? Are you trying to kill us?"

Moses grew annoyed. "You always complain! Hasn't God promised you a great land to call your home? A land of water, of green valleys and hills? Hasn't He promised you all of this?" "If God provides you with water, will you stop whining?" "Well, yes," Dathan said. "But there's no water around here!"

"See how God loves you!" Moses struck a boulder with his staff. Water gushed forth in the form of a waterfall. The people celebrated, dashing forward to the precious water.

Nathan walked up to Moses.

"You know, we could use some food, too. Any ideas?"

Moses rolled his eyes and walked away in disgust.

That night, alone in the desert, Moses sat before the pillar of fire. "Lord, these people are driving me mad, I just don't understand what you want me to do."

God said "I have heard the murmurings

of Israel. Come morning, I will rain food from the Heavens."

Moses thanked the Lord and in the morning, it was so. On the ground lay countless small cakes, sparkling like the frost. The people were astonished. They tasted them. They tasted like honey. The people rejoiced.

Moses watched the Hebrews collect the cakes.

"This is the bread the Lord has given you," he said. "It is manna. Bread from Heaven. Take it. Eat it. Let your stomachs be full!"

After a few days of marching, the people again grew restless. As Moses rested under a palm tree, Dathan led a group of complainers up to Moses. "Why hasn't God given us any meat, It's always manna, manna, manna," Moses stalked off, holding his tongue.

He sat down before the fire pillar. "Now, they want meat," Moses sighed. "Lord? There is no meat out here."

The voice of God emerged from the cloud. "Is my power doubted?

Tell the people they shall have food to go on. I will give them their meat."

The people cheered. Moses walked off, seeking solitude.

He sat on a rock when a young, strapping boy named Joshua approached him. Moses smiled at the boy.

"Ah, Joshua, my young general."

"I'm no general, Moses," the boy blushed.

"One day you will be," Moses replied. The boy was stunned. "Really?"

"Now, would you tell Aaron and Miriam I'd like to speak to them?" The boy ran off.

"Yes, sir."

Soon, Aaron and Miriam were sitting across from Moses. Miriam told Moses that he had promised the Hebrews too much. Moses was saddened. He remembered when both Aaron and Miriam believed. When they had faith. He faced the sky.

A fierce wind buffeted both Miriam and Aaron, who clung to each other in fear. The voice of God whispered to them both. God said that, while he spoke to everyone who believed in Him,

Moses was the only man He spoke to face to face. God chose Moses to be His servant because he was the most humble man on Earth.

The wind subsided. Aaron and Miriam were speechless. "Never forget God's plan," Moses advised them.

At that point, a noise disturbed them. They all looked up and saw an endless flock of quail heading for their encampment. Normally, the little birds would not be out in the desert but God had promised His Children meat and, thus, had delivered on His promise.

Soon, the long caravan approached Mount Sinai, following the cloud pillar. Suddenly, the pillar of cloud disappeared. In the lead of the travelers, Moses, Miriam and Aaron stared up at the mountain.

"What is this strange place?" Miriam asked.

"It's the place God first appeared to me," said Moses. "God wants me there, again."

A dark, purple cloud appeared over the mountain, covering its highest peak. Thunder roared. Lightning flashed. From within the cloud appeared the flickering shadows of a large flame. It illuminated the cloud. From within the cloud came the sound of a deafening trumpet. The people cowered, some covering their ears. Moses smiled. "Can't you hear it? It is the voice of God! Do not be fearful!"

"One day, you will all be able to open your hearts to His voice.

 The Desert Journey

Now, I must go up on the mountain and talk with God."

"Be careful, Moses," Aaron advised.

"Aaron, watch over the people," Moses answered. "They may grow restless." Aaron nodded and Moses marched off towards the mountain.

The thick purple cloud grew nearer, illuminated by a bright red glow.

Moses turned toward the dark cloud, the flame flickering within it. Moses had only his faith to guide him.

Below Moses, at the foot of Mount Sinai, the Children of Israel were losing their faith.

The Ten Commandments

With Moses gone so long, the people grew nervous. The rebels were led by Dathan, who declared: "Moses has deserted us! He's been up there forever! He's dead, I tell you. Dead!"

Dathan ran up to Aaron, grabbing him by the robe. "Aaron, make us a god! A real god! A god who will lead us to the Promised Land!"

The crowd cheered. But Aaron refused. A few of Dathan's bullies surrounded Aaron. "Make us a God," Dathan threatened. "Or die on that mountain with your brother. Or die down here... with your sister."

The people cheered as Dathan ordered them about. "Break off the gold rings from the ears of your wives and your daughters! Bring them to Aaron! Get all that Egyptian gold! All their silver! Their jewelry!"

"Aaron will make us a real god! A Golden Calf! Who needs Moses and his invisible God! Not me! Not you!"

Muttering "May God forgive me," Aaron slowly began work on crafting Dathan's Golden Calf. Within days, Aaron had finished the abomination.

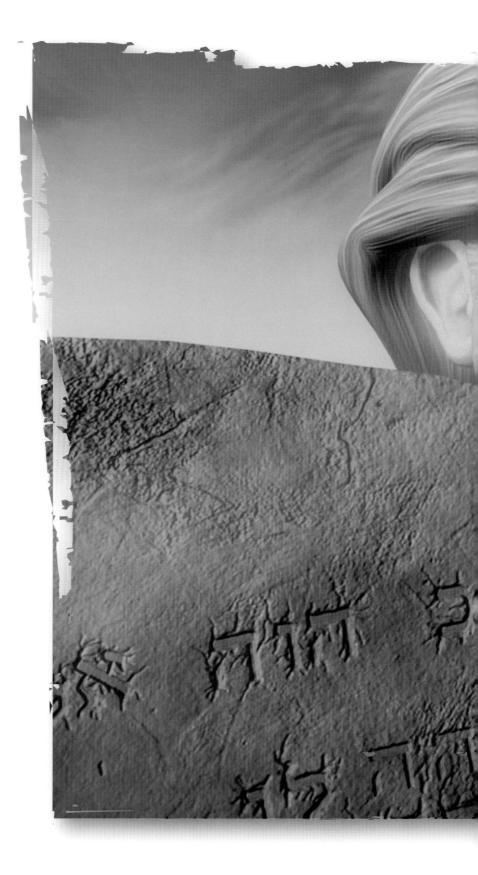

et's dance and sing and give praise to our new god!" Dathan shouted. "It's a god we can all see face to face! Not like Moses' private God!"

Some of the Hebrews began to play instruments. Others danced.

On Mount Sinai, the fire grew and burst all around Moses.

Moses was suddenly embraced by a strong wind. The voice of God came to him.

"Now listen, Moses," God said. "I give to you the way to live. I give you my Ten Commandments. Remember them. Teach them. Teach them for the rest of your life."

The slabs of stone containing the commandments slowly emerged in the form of two tablets. They floated down into Moses' arms. Moses gazed upwards. "Thank you, God. Thank you."

Clutching the tablets, Moses hurried down the mountain.

At the foot of the mountain, the Children of Israel, led by Dathan, drank and danced and played songs around the Golden Calf. In the middle of the festivities, Moses emerged on a cliff above the celebrants. He stared down at his people, horrified and angry.
Thunder roared.

The partygoers stopped, looking up at the ledge.

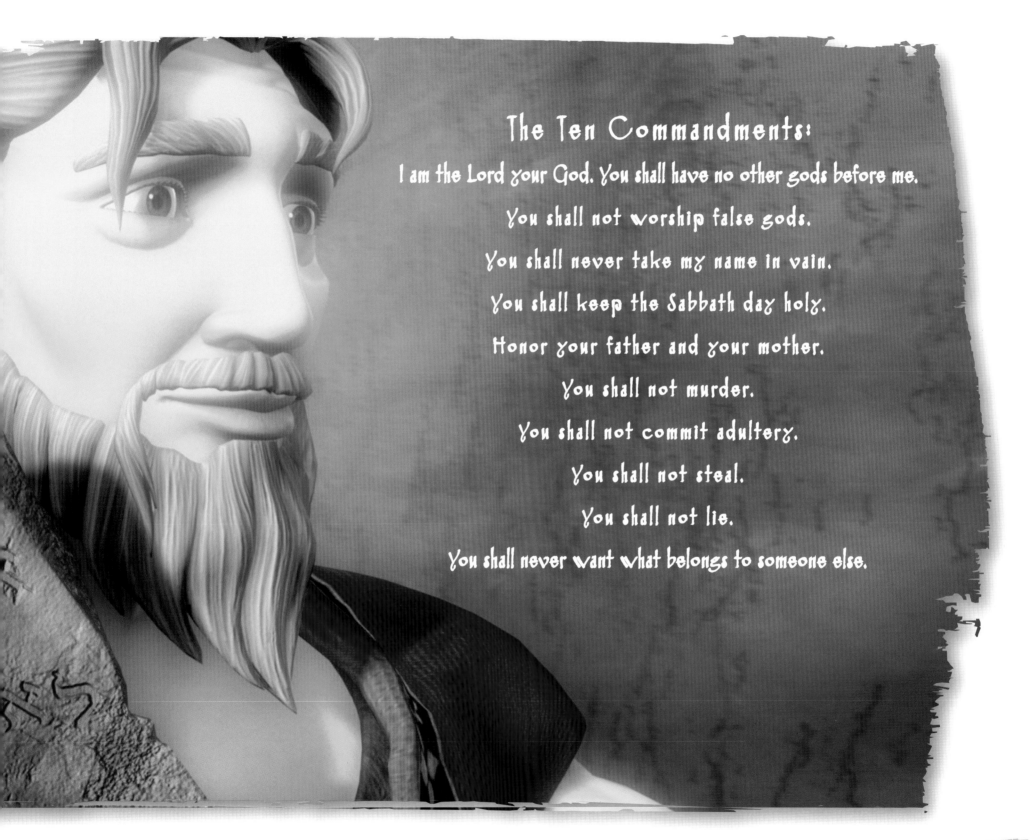

The Ten Commandments:

I am the Lord your God. You shall have no other gods before me.

You shall not worship false gods.

You shall never take my name in vain.

You shall keep the Sabbath day holy.

Honor your father and your mother.

You shall not murder.

You shall not commit adultery.

You shall not steal.

You shall not lie.

You shall never want what belongs to someone else.

Moses looked down from the precipice, tablets in hand. "This is how you repay the Lord?" he shouted. "He brought you out of slavery! He led you across the desert! He parted the seas to let you live! And yet, you turn from him to a false god? A god of your own creation?"

A saddened Moses stared down at the Children of Israel and whispered. "Don't you realize He loves you?"

He raised the tablets. "He gave these to us. His Commandments."

The people were torn.

Moses addressed them sternly. "All who believe in the Lord, all who are on His side. Come to Him! Walk towards me."

With the faithful standing beneath him, Moses stared at Dathan and the unbelievers, huddled around the Golden Calf. Moses raised the tablets above his head, almost snarling. "Today, you will witness the judgment of the Lord!"

Moses hurled the sacred tablets down towards the disbelievers.

 The Ten Commandments

They landed and shattered, exploding in front of the Golden Calf. The earth beneath the golden idol split in two. Plumes of flame shot up, as if from a volcano. The Golden Calf as well as Dathan and the unbelievers plunged down into the fiery pit. The earth slowly came back together, healing itself.

Later, the faithful restored the camp as Moses and Aaron talked.

Aaron was worried. "God's laws! They're destroyed."

Moses only smiled. "I'll go back to the mountain. God will replace the tablets."

After Moses went back up to the mountain, Aaron faced his workers. "We must construct an Ark. An Ark to house the tablets. And we must construct a Tabernacle, a tent, so that God may dwell in our midst."

When Moses returned with two more tablets, the caravan began to move across the barren desert, once again. Soon, however, the people began to complain, again.

Moses met with God in the meeting tent every day, a huge cloud hovering over it. The travelers began to lose patience with Moses.

Inside the Tabernacle, Moses listened to the voice of a frustrated God. "How long will these people disobey me?" God asked. "How long will they turn their backs on all I have done for them? Perhaps, I should just abandon them!"

Moses pleaded, "Please, pardon the sins of these people because of Your unfailing love, just as You've forgiven them since freeing them from Egypt."

The Lord was silent. Finally, God said: "I will pardon them, Moses. But not one of them will see the Promised Land. They will all wander the wilderness until the last of their generation is gone. Their children and their children's children will make the final journey without them."

The caravan continued onward. But the sins of the Children of Israel would cause them to wander in the wilderness for forty years until all the older generation that would not believe in the way of the Lord perished.

The Promised Land

The years went by and more and more of the old travelers died. Moses' sister, Miriam, died peacefully in her sleep. Soon, Moses' brother Aaron became too sick to walk. Moses visited his brother in Aaron's tent.

"Are you in pain?" Moses asked.

Aaron smiled. "No. I'll be seeing God's face, soon."

Moses put his hand upon Aaron's. "You've been the best of brothers, Aaron. You helped me. Stayed by my side."

Aaron chuckled. "We really caused Pharaoh some problems, remember?"

Moses found himself laughing, too. He wiggled his shepherd's staff. "The snake?"

Aaron giggled like a young boy. "And those flies? I think the flies were my favorite. Oh, how Pharaoh hated those flies. God has a great sense of humor."

Staring at his dying brother, Moses grew sorrowful. Aaron patted Moses' hand. "Don't be sad, Moses. We were blessed. We were chosen by God. Soon, our people will see The Promised Land. That is a great thing."

Moses leaned over and kissed Aaron on the forehead. Aaron smiled and sighed. Then, he was gone.

Within days, the caravan came to a special place, next to a great mountain, Mount Nebo. Behind them lay the desert. Before them, just beyond a river, was a green, fertile land stretching as far as the eye could see. It was the lush land of

The Promised Land

milk and honey God had promised. The Children of Israel stared at the Promised Land and cheered.

"Children of Israel," Moses announced. "God has told me I must die in this land. He told me I would never cross the River Jordan with you. My friend Joshua will lead you, now. You will all cross over and live in The Promised Land and the Lord will be with you all. He will watch over you, you will lack nothing.

You will have food! You will have homes! Your fields will sprout bountiful harvests! But you should never forget this journey. Never forget God's words. Keep them in your hearts. Never turn your back on a stranger. For, we were all strangers in Egypt. Remember all that He has given us. He is merciful. And, if you sin? Ask his forgiveness. He will grant it to you. Why? Because He loves us all."

The crowd cheered as Moses raised his staff. "It's time that you cross the River Jordan! Go on! Onto the Promised Land!"

Moses turned to Joshua. "Lead them, my general. Lead them!"

Moses smiled, watching the people go. He turned and faced Mount Nebo.

He heard a soft voice. It was a voice he knew well. "Coming, Lord. Coming," Moses said.

Moses climbed to the top of Mount Nebo. He stared down and grinned. The Chosen People, led by Joshua, were crossing the River Jordan and heading for The Promised Land.

Moses faced the heavens, staff in hand. "I'm ready, Lord."

Large, white clouds gathered above Moses.

The voice of God whispered. "This is your place, Moses. This is your place."

The top of Mount Nebo shimmered with sunlight. Moses died on that mountain-top. Yet, no man has found his resting place to this day. In all the years since then, there has never been a prophet like Moses. Moses, a humble man of great faith. Moses. The man who God chose to lead the Chosen People out of slavery. Moses. The friend of God, whom God met with face to face.